EYE TO EYE WITH DOGS

COCKER SPANIELS

Lynn M. Stone

Rourke
Publishing LLC
Vero Beach, Florida 32964

www.rourkepublishing.com

PHOTO CREDITS: All photos © Lynn M. Stone

Editor: Meg Greve

Cover and page design by Nicola Stratford

Library of Congress Cataloging-in-Publication Data

Stone, Lynn M.
  Cocker spaniels / Lynn M. Stone.   26650
    p. cm. -- (Eye to eye with dogs)
  Includes index.
  ISBN 978-1-60472-362-5
  1. Cocker spaniels--Juvenile literature. I. Title.
  SF429.C55S76 2009
  --dc22
                                    2008012975

Printed in the USA

CG/CG

Rourke Publishing

www.rourkepublishing.com – rourke@rourkepublishing.com
Post Office Box 3328, Vero Beach, FL 32964

Table of Contents

A high, domed skull is typical of American cocker spaniels.

Cocker Spaniels

The cocker spaniel is one of North America's most popular and loved dog **breeds**. Cocker spaniels are small dogs with long, thick fur. Cocker spaniel owners especially prize their dogs' cheery personalities.

AMERICAN COCKER SPANIEL FACTS
Weight: 24 to 32 pounds (11 to 15 kilograms)
Height: 14 to 15 inches (36 to 38 centimeters)
Country of Origin: United States
Life Span: 12 to 15 years

ENGLISH COCKER SPANIEL FACTS
Weight: 26 to 34 pounds (12 to 15 kilograms)
Height: 15 to 17 inches (38 to 43 centimeters)
Country of Origin: England
Life Span: 13 to 14 years

The English cocker spaniel is usually slightly larger than its American cousin.

The cocker earned its name in England many years ago because of its usefulness in hunting **woodcock**, a sandpiper-like bird. The cocker's job was to find the woodcock by scent, then **flush** it for the hunter.

Sporting people still use English cockers frequently as field dogs.

The American cocker spaniel remains one of the most popular North American dog breeds.

Many dogs are spaniels. The Canadian Kennel Club, for example, recognizes 12 different spaniel breeds, including English springer spaniels, Irish water spaniels, and Welsh springer spaniels.

The two cocker spaniel breeds, American and English, are the smallest spaniels. The American breed, known simply as cocker spaniel by the American Kennel Club, is also one of America's favorite purebred dogs.

An English cocker enjoys the company of its young human companion.

American cockers outnumber their English cousins in the United States and Canada. In the past ten years however, the English cocker has been gaining in popularity in North America. Outside North America, English cockers are much more common than American cockers.

The American Kennel Club recognizes both cocker spaniel breeds as sporting dogs. By tradition, cocker spaniels are fine hunters.

Both the American and Canadian Kennel Clubs recognize the English and American cockers as sporting breeds.

Many English cocker owners still train their dogs for fieldwork, such as hunting and **tracking**. American cocker spaniels receive training for fieldwork far less often.

The English cocker's fine nose makes it an ideal breed for tracking scents in competition.

Looks

A cocker spaniel is a sturdy, compact dog with a deep chest. The American cocker spaniel has a more boxy **muzzle** and higher skull. Many describe its large eyes as soft. They help give the cocker its cuddly good looks.

A cheery personality makes cocker spaniels beloved pets.

Americans dock the tails of many dog breeds, including the cocker spaniel, boxers, and German shorthaired pointers.

One cocker spaniel does not look like the next. A cocker's fur may be any solid color or a combination of colors, like black with tan trim.

Both cocker breeds have thick, wavy hair and long, furry, floppy ears. American and English cockers in the United States have short tails only because Americans usually **dock** their tails.

The American breed has a shorter back and a smaller, rounder head than the English cocker. The English cocker has a flatter skull and a longer muzzle.

Cockers enjoy being outside, especially on a mild spring day.

The short muzzle on this cocker spaniel reveals it as an American.

Cocker Spaniels of the Past

The spaniel family of dogs probably began in Spain. A record of a *spanyell* dates back to 1368. Eventually, dog owners brought the spaniel to England.

English breeders developed several types of spaniels, including this English springer spaniel.

For many years, there were two groups of spaniels in England, land spaniels and water spaniels. In the late 1800s, **breeders** divided the land spaniels into two groups, toys and cockers. The smaller toy types proved to be excellent companions. Cockers continued to be sporting dogs.

The British used cockers primarily as hunting dogs.

The American cocker spaniel has a shorter back and smaller, rounder head than the English cocker.

Around 1880, importers sent English cockers to the United States. American breeders slowly began to make small changes in the cocker's appearance.

They tended to choose the smallest English cockers as parents. Over time, the Americans developed a smaller breed with a somewhat different shape.

Both cocker breeds can usually tolerate both cold and hot weather.

In 1946, the American Kennel Club recognized two separate breeds, the American and the English. The Canadian Kennel Club also recognizes both breeds.

The Dog for You?

A cocker spaniel's merry, playful personality has long been one of its charms. A cocker spaniel loves the outdoors, but needs to be with the family indoors as well.

Cockers are small enough to be comfortable in almost any home. However, even **homebody** cockers need exercise, such as a walk. Cockers also do well in **agility** and obedience training.

A romp helps keep a cocker spaniel healthy and content.

Cockers in dog shows need plenty of hair care, including almost daily grooming. Most owners do not enter their dogs in shows. They often clip their dogs' hair for the sake of comfort and easier care.

Cockers may bark a great deal, and they can easily gain too much weight without proper care.

Like other highly popular dogs, American cocker spaniels have been bred in large numbers. Breeders have not always been careful about selecting parent dogs. As a result, an American cocker could have any of several health problems such as skin lesions or deafness.

This fine example of an American cocker spaniel pup resulted from a breeder's careful choice of parents.

A Note about Dogs

Puppies are cute and cuddly, but only after serious thought should anybody buy one. Puppies, after all, grow up.

A dog will require more than love and patience. It will need healthy food, exercise, grooming, medical care, and a warm, safe place to live.

A dog can be your best friend, but you need to be its best friend, too.

Choosing the right breed for you requires homework. For more information about buying and owning a dog, contact the American Kennel Club or the Canadian Kennel Club.

Glossary

agility (AJ-il-i-tee): the ability to perform certain athletic tasks, such as leaping through a hoop

breeds (BREEDS): particular kinds of domestic animals within a larger, closely related group, such as the cocker spaniel within the dog group

breeders (BREED-urz): those who keep adult dogs and raise their pups, especially those who do so regularly and with great care

dock (DOK): to remove a section of tail, leaving a very short tail

flush (FLUHSH): to chase from hiding; to chase into flight

homebody (HOME-bod-ee): one who likes to remain close to home

muzzle (MUHZ-uhl): the nose and jaw portion of a dog's head

tracking (TRAK-ing): following a trail by scent

woodcock (WUD-kok): a sandpiper-like bird of moist woodlands

Index

Further Reading

Gray, Susan H. *Cocker Spaniels*. Child's World, 2008.
Miller, Connie Colwell. *Cocker Spaniels*. Pebble Books, 2007.
Murray, Julie. *Cocker Spaniels*. ABDO, 2004.

Website to Visit

www.akc.org/breeds/cocker_spaniel
www.asc-cockerspaniel.org
www.ecsca.org

About the Author

Lynn M. Stone is a widely-published wildlife and domestic animal photographer and the author of more than 500 children's books. His book *Box Turtles* was chosen as an Outstanding Science Trade Book and Selectors' Choice for 2008 by the Science Committee of the National Science Teachers' Association and the Children's Book Council.